LOVE, IDENTITY, & PURPOSE

IN CHRIST

1ST-3RD GRADE LEADER'S GUIDE

All scriptures are taken from The Holy Bible, New King James Version (NKJV). Copyright © 1979, 1980, 1982 by Thomas Nelson, Inc. Used by permission. All rights reserved.

Curriculum & print design by Megan Parks
Graphic design by Michal Edridge

First paperback edition October 2021

To order additional copies, or for more information, please visit:
J. Terry Moore
4041 Marsh Lane
Carrollton, TX 75007
www.jterrymoore.org

Updated & Printed 11/2022

ISBN 979-8-9873004-0-4

INTRODUCTION

From the very beginning, God showed us His LOVE for us, our IDENTITY in Him, and our PURPOSE on earth. Jesus came to restore us back to what God showed us in the very beginning.

The lessons in this book are adapted from Pastor Terry Moore's equipping series, specifically the "Love, Identity, & Purpose" manual. These lessons are designed to teach students about God's original plan and design for them.

CONTENTS

Scripture: Genesis 1:27
Lesson Length: 45-50 minutes

CREATED IN GOD'S IMAGE

Intro
(3-5 mins)

Say: "As humans, sometimes we struggle with knowing how much we are loved by God and our identity in Him, which is who we are as a person. God knew that we would need answers for these areas of life. In the very first book of the Bible, Genesis, He shows us everything we need to know about our love and identity in Him."

Introduce Today's Scripture: "So God created man in His own image; in the image of God He created him; male and female He created them." Genesis 1:27

Create-A-Twin Activity
(6-8 mins)

Say: "If you were to create another person "in your image," meaning they are exactly like you, what type of personality traits would they have? Make sure you give them all of the personality traits that you have!"

Have students draw or write down their person's personality traits, and then have them share what they came up with.

> "So God created man in His own image; in the image of God He created him; male and female He created them."
>
> Genesis 1:27

- Create your own list/drawing to share. For example: "I drew my person with a soccer ball because they'd be athletic. I also drew them with a big heart, because they'd be a loving sister, just like me."
- For younger students, you can sit in a circle and go around and have them share one trait that their person would have.

Lesson

(8-10 mins)

Say: "Just like you gave your same traits to your made-up person so they would be just like you, God created us to be just like Him! Genesis 1:26-27 tells us that we are created in His image, which means we were created to be like Him. It is important that we know all of the traits of God, because it will show us who we are, as creations of God!

The most important trait for us to know is that God is love. In 1 John 4:8, it says, 'He who does not love does not know God, for God is love.' This verse tells us that God is love, which means He's full of love, and is whole being is made of love. If God created us to be just like Him, then He created us in love, just like Him, because He loves us so much!

2

We can also look to Jesus as an example of how much God loves us. In John 3:16, it says, 'For God so loved the world that He gave His only begotten Son.' God showed us how much He loves us by having Jesus die on the cross for us. Because Jesus is the son of God, we can also look to Jesus to see who we are as creations of God.

In Luke 3:22 we can see how God feels about Jesus. It says, 'A voice came from heaven which said, 'You are my beloved Son; in You I am well pleased.'' God thinks the same way about us! He calls us his beloved, deeply loved, sons and daughters, and He is very pleased with us. So now we know that our identity, like Christ, is that we are loved by the Father and we are pleasing to Him. When God says He is pleased with us, it means that it brings Him joy to be our Heavenly Father!

When we accept Christ as our savior, God sees us just like Christ, His beloved son, who is perfect and deeply loved by the Father. Some other verses in the Bible, like in Ephesians, tell us other loving traits that God gives us through Jesus. It says we are 'without blame, accepted, chosen from the beginning, God's family, rooted in love, holy, and blessed with every spiritual blessing.' There are so many wonderful traits that God gave us when He created us in His image!"

Memory Verse
(8-10 mins)

"So God created man in His own image; in the image of God He created him; male and female He created them." Genesis 1:27

- Use hand motions each time you memorize the words of the verse together. ***For younger students, you can memorize a smaller portion of the verse.**
- Optional Game: Write the verse on a chalkboard, dry erase board, or create slides with the verse. Say it together. Erase one word. Say it again. Erase another word and say it out loud together. Keep going until the whole verse is erased.
- Extension Games (optional): Split into 2 teams and race to see which team can have each member recite the verse the fastest

or recite 'round robin' style with each student taking turns saying one word from the verse until they complete the entire verse together.

Directions: Have students draw a picture of themselves and surround it with symbols and words that describe who they are as children created in God's own image.
- Option: Print and cut the Identity Printout (pg. 6) for students to glue the words to their poster.

Example Identity Words: son, daughter, beloved, deeply loved, pleasing to God, God's family, chosen from the beginning, holy, without blame, blessed with every spiritual blessing, created in God's image

Craft: Identity Poster (10-12 mins)

Give students a copy of lesson handout on pg. 5.

Say: "This week we are going to declare God's love for us, since we were created, in love, by Him. It is important that we know that God is love and just how much God loves us."

Say Declaration and Prayer together.

Weekly Declaration: God created me in His own image. God is love, therefore, I am created and surrounded by His love.

Prayer: Father, I love You so much and I thank You for loving me! I pray that I will fully understand Your love with my whole heart and mind. Help me know that I am accepted and deeply loved because of what Jesus did at the cross for me. In Jesus' name, amen!

Weekly Prayer and Declaration (3-5 mins)

Lesson 1:
Created in God's Image

Verse
"So God created man in His own image; in the image of God He created him; male and female He created them."
Genesis 1:27

Declaration
God created me in His own image. God is love, therefore, I am created and surrounded by His love.

Prayer
Father, I love You so much and I thank You for loving me! I pray that I will fully understand Your love with my whole heart and mind. Help me know that I am accepted and deeply loved because of what Jesus did at the cross for me. In Jesus' name, amen!

*Use to make copies for students

Daughter	Son
DEEPLY LOVED	BELOVED
God's Family	Pleasing to God
Holy	Chosen from the beginning
blessed with every spiritual blessing	Without Blame
Christ-like	Created in God's Image

*Use to make copies for students

Scripture: Ephesians 1:5
Lesson Length: 45-50 minutes

THE FALL AND THE CROSS

Review
(4-6 mins)

Review last week's verse and declaration:
"So God created man in His own image; in the image of God He created him; male and female He created them." Genesis 1:27

- Show verse on the screen for those who weren't here last week.
- Ask students if they were able to memorize the verse. You can ask students to show a thumbs up or thumbs down to if they were able to memorize it and then ask students to recite it as a class, or recite it in groups of 2-3 if most already memorized it.
- Next, recite last week's Declaration together as a class:
  God created me in His own image. God is love, therefore, I am created and surrounded by His love.

Ask: "What does it mean to be created in God's image?" *Let 1-2 students share.*

Say: "God created us to be like Him."

Ask: "Share one trait with the person closest to you that God gave you when He created you in His image." *Give 5-10 seconds for students to share. Ex: son, daughter, deeply loved, etc.*

God has "predestined us to adoption as sons [and daughters] by Jesus Christ to Himself, according to the good pleasure of His will."

Ephesians 1:5

Introduce Today's Scripture: God has "predestined us to adoption as sons [and daughters] by Jesus Christ to Himself, according to the good pleasure of His will." Ephesians 1:5

Say: "Now that we know that God created us in His own image, it is helpful to know what causes us to have doubts about who we are and just how much God loves us. In Genesis 3, we see where these feelings all started. It tells us about 'the fall of man' that happened with Adam and Eve."

Ask: "What do you know about Adam and Eve?" *Give students 5-10 seconds to think of their answer. Have them share with the person closest to them. Then, ask 1-3 students to share with the group.*

Say: "When God made Adam and Eve, they disobeyed God by eating the apple which caused the 'fall of man.' The 'fall of man' refers to the time that sin entered the world. It was the first time man disobeyed God, which is sin. Sin is when we do not obey, or follow, God's word. Sin caused man to be separated from God, which gave man an 'orphan spirit.' An orphan means somebody that is without parents. Because of Jesus, we are no longer orphans."

8

Memory Verse

(8-10 mins)

God has "predestined us to adoption as sons [and daughters] by Jesus Christ to Himself, according to the good pleasure of His will." Ephesians 1:5

- Use hand motions each time you memorize the words of the verse together. ***For younger students, you can memorize a smaller portion of the verse.**
- Optional Game: Write the verse on a chalkboard, dry erase board, or create slides with the verse. Say it together. Erase one word. Say it again. Erase another word and say it out loud together. Keep going until the whole verse is erased.
- Extension Games (optional): Split into 2 teams and race to see which team can have each member recite the verse the fastest or recite 'round robin' style with each student taking turns saying one word from the verse until they complete the entire verse together.

Lesson

(8-10 mins)

Say: "An orphan is described as someone without parents. Man became like an orphan because sin entered the world and separated man from God, the Father. When sin causes us to feel like orphans, and we don't know how much God the Father loves us. It can make us question our identity, which is who we are as a person. Sin gets in the way and makes us forget that we were created in God's own image.

Jesus came to take sin out of the way. Jesus died on the cross so we can live out God's original plan for us as sons and daughters, which He planned before 'the fall of man.' We no longer have to feel like orphans because of our sins that separated us from God. At the cross, Jesus died for our sins so we would no longer be separated from the love of Father God and no longer be orphans.

- Extension (optional): Ask again if somebody can remind us what an 'orphan' is.

The Bible says, in Ephesians 1:5, that God has 'predestined us to adoption as sons [and daughters] by Jesus Christ to Himself, according to the good pleasure of His will.' When you are 'predestined' for something, it means that it was planned way before you were born. So, we can see in this verse that God's original plan from the beginning of time was that we are to live as sons and daughters with Him as our Father.

The verse also says it happened 'by Jesus Christ to Himself,' which shows us that Jesus' death on the cross was what fixed 'the fall of man' that occurred with Adam and Eve, and returned us back to God's sons and daughters. Because Jesus died for you and for me, we can now live as sons and daughters instead of orphans.

To make it even better, the verse ends by saying, 'according to the good pleasure of His will,' which shows us that it brings God pleasure and joy to be our Father because He loves us so much! Remember, God is Love!

It is important that we understand and embrace in our hearts the love of the Father and our identity in Christ as sons and daughters, because God wants to bless us and be in close relationship with us. In Romans 8:15, it says, 'For you did not receive the spirit of bondage again to fear, but you received the Spirit of adoption by whom we cry out, 'Abba, Father!'' The verse shows us that we are no longer orphans that are connected to, or stuck living with, 'the fall of man.' We can now call to 'Abba, Father,' which means our daddy God, for help because we are His sons and daughters.

Think about how much your parents want you to be happy and want to keep you safe. Our Heavenly God wants to bless us and keep us safe even more so, because He loves us so much. He wants us to know He is our loving Father, who is so pleased with us, and wants us to be safe and close to Him."

Activity: Comic Strip

(8-10 mins)

Materials: Comic strips v1, v2, or v3 (pg. 14-16)

Objective: Students will create a comic strip showing God creating man in His own image, "the fall of man," and how Jesus brought us back as sons and daughters at the cross.

Directions: Help each student choose appropriate comic strip version - v1, v2, v3 - to work on based on their age level.

Say: "Remember, sin entered the world during 'the fall of man,' which took place with Adam and Eve. Sin caused man to be separated from God, and gave man an 'orphan spirit.' Jesus entered the world so that we would no longer be orphans. We are now sons and daughters of God, our loving Father through Jesus!

Draw a comic strip showing the 'fall of man' with Adam and Eve, and how Jesus saved us at the cross to make us sons and daughters of God."

Weekly Prayer and Declaration

(3-5 mins)

Give students a copy of lesson handout on pg. 13.

Say: "This week, we are going to declare ourselves as God's sons and daughters and remind ourselves that it brings God joy to be our Father."

Say Declaration and Prayer together.

Weekly Declaration: Jesus died on the cross so I don't have to feel like an orphan, separated from God's love. I am now a son/daughter of God the Father, because it brings God joy to be my Heavenly Father.

Prayer: Father, thank You for choosing me as Your son/daughter

before I was born. Thank You that sin no longer separates me from You because of what Jesus did at the cross for me. I pray that I can continue to know Your love for me as Your son/daughter. In Jesus' name, amen!

Lesson 2:
The Fall and
The Cross

Verse
"God has predestined us to adoption as sons and daughters by Jesus Christ to Himself, according to the good pleasure of His will."
Ephesians 1:5

Declaration
Jesus died on the cross so I don't have to feel like an orphan, separated from God's love. I am now a son/daughter of God the Father, because it brings God joy to be my Heavenly Father.

Prayer
Father, thank You for choosing me as Your son/daughter before I was born. Thank You that sin no longer separates me from You because of what Jesus did at the cross for me. I pray that I can continue to know Your love for me as Your son/daughter. In Jesus' name, amen!

*Use to make copies for students

COMIC TITLE: **The Fall and the Cross**

Adam and Eve ate the apple which brought sin and separation from God.	Jesus came so we could be adopted as sons and daughters of God, our loving Father!

COMIC TITLE:

God created man in His own image.	Adam and Eve disobeyed God and ate from the tree, which caused man to be separated from God.
Jesus entered the world to take care of sin so that man would no longer be separated from God.	We are now adopted as sons and daughters through Christ Jesus. God is our loving Father!

COMIC TITLE:

_____

Scripture: Ephesians 3:17-19
Lesson Length: 45-50 minutes

THE LOVE OF THE FATHER

Review
(3-5 mins)

Review last week's verse and declaration:
God has "predestined us to adoption as sons [and daughters] by Jesus Christ to Himself, according to the good pleasure of His will." Ephesians 1:5

- Show verse on the screen for those who weren't here last week.
- Ask students if they were able to memorize the verse. You can ask students to show a thumbs up or thumbs down to if they were able to memorize it and then ask students to recite it as a class, or recite it in groups of 2-3 if most already memorized it.
- Next, recite last week's Declaration together as a class:
  Jesus died on the cross so I don't have to feel like an orphan, separated from God's love. I am now a son/daughter of God the Father, because it brings God joy to be my Heavenly Father.

"That you, being rooted and grounded in love, may be able to comprehend [...] the width and length and depth and height- to know the love of Christ which passes knowledge; that you may be filled with all the fullness of God."

Ephesians 3:17-19

Introduce Today's Scripture: "That you, being rooted and grounded in love, may be able to comprehend [...] the width and length and depth and height- to know the love of Christ which passes knowledge; that you may be filled with all the fullness of God." Ephesians 3:17-19

- Optional: use tape measure to act out "width, length, depth, height" while you introduce verse.

Say: "The love of God, our Father, is one of the most important things we can ever know in our minds and in our hearts. By knowing why Christ died for us at the cross, we are planted like flowers, and rooted in the Father's love."

Ask: "Who knows what 'Roots' are?" *Let 1-2 students answer. Show a picture of a flower with roots, if possible.*

Say: "Roots are the part of a flower that attach it to the soil in the ground and keep it firmly planted. The verse tells us to be planted in God's love, so we can be filled with God's fullness. God is love, so to be 'filled with God's fullness,' is to be filled with God's love. When you're filled with God's love, you will be able to face any challenges in life."

Activity: Rooted in Love

(8-10 mins)

Objective: Demonstrate how being rooted in God's love (soil) keeps us (flowers) secure in life's challenges.

Materials: Buckets, Plastic Flowers, Handheld Fans (or have students fold paper accordion fans), Soil (optional substitution: green flower staging styrofoam or pebbles)

Directions: Each student will get one plastic flower. Have buckets of soil spread out across the table for students to plant their flowers in. Have the children fan their flowers and watch how they stand firm in the soil (Father's love).
*option to use green flower staging styrofoam or pebbles for a less messy demonstration.

Say: "The Father's love is like the soil that protects and helps flowers grow. Imagine that you're the flower, and you're planted in the Father's love."
Demonstrate planting your flower in the soil. Leave it shallow so you can later demonstrate being more deeply rooted in God's love. Then have students plant their flowers.

Say: "Sometimes in life we deal with challenging situations, like having an argument with a friend, an injury, or feeling like we don't fit in. Tough situations are like wind that blow us around and try to make us forget how much God loves us. Watch what happens when we're planted in God's love and the wind from a tough situation tries to blow us over."
Use a fan to blow on your flower. Then give students the opportunity to use a fan to blow on their own flower, or have them physically blow on their own flower.

Ask: "How does the soil help the flower?" *Give students an opportunity to answer.*

Say: "When we are planted and rooted in God's love, like the flower in the soil, those tough winds can't knock us down or pull us away from God's love. We can use God's love to keep us safe. Now watch what happens when I plant my flower even deeper

19

into God's love."

Dig your flower deeper into the soil, and demonstrate using the fan.

Ask: "Did anybody notice a difference when my flower was planted deeper?" *Let 1-2 students answer.*

Say: "When my flower was rooted deeply in the love of the Father, the wind could barely move it. That is how we want to be in our lives so that we can easily face any strong wind, or tough situation, that tries to blow us over."
Give students a chance to dig their flowers deeper and blow on them, if there is enough time

Clean up and start the next activity.

"That you, being rooted and grounded in love, may be able to comprehend ... what is the width and length and depth and height- to know the love of Christ which passes knowledge; that you may be filled with all the fullness of God."
Ephesians 3:17-19

Memory Verse (8-10 mins)

- Use hand motions each time you memorize the words of the verse together. ***For younger students, you can memorize a smaller portion of the verse.**
- Optional Game: Write the verse on a chalkboard, dry erase board, or create slides with the verse. Say it together. Erase one word. Say it again. Erase another word and say it out loud together. Keep going until the whole verse is erased.
- Extension Games (optional): Split into 2 teams and race to see which team can have each member recite the verse the fastest or recite 'round robin' style with each student taking turns saying one word from the verse until they complete the entire verse together.

Say: "To understand God's love, and plant ourselves in it, we must understand why Jesus died at the cross for us. We saw in last week's verse that Jesus came so we would no longer be orphans, and could be sons and daughters of God."

Ask: "Why do you think He chose to do that for us?" *Let students share their answer with the person closest to them, and then have 1-2 students share with the group.*

Say: "The Bible tells us in John 3:16, 'For God so loved the world, that He gave His only begotten Son that whoever believes in Him should not perish but have everlasting life.' God SO loves us, and that is why He gave his only Son, Jesus, to die for us. It is NOTHING we did to deserve it, but ONLY because God loves us so much.

Another way to think of His love is in Romans 5:8: 'God demonstrates His own love toward us, in that while we were still sinners, Christ died for us.' This verse shows us that it is nothing we do that made Him want to die for us. We were, and still are sinners, yet Jesus chose to die for us anyways. The ONLY reason Christ died for us sinners is because God loves us so much. That is an amazing love!

To understand God's love better, we also have to understand exactly what happened at the cross. Jesus was the payment for the sins of the entire world, which included your sin and my sin. He paid for our sins and took all of the wrath and anger of God for those sins on the cross. Because God dealt with all of sin at the cross, He chooses to no longer see our sins today. Jesus paid for all sin, so God will never be angry with us for sin. Remember, God IS love. It is who and what He is; He acts in love and gives love only. He doesn't love some of the things we say, think, or do, but He only shows love to us because that is who He is. He chooses to forget our sins and loves us as His sons and daughters.

Because we can't do anything to earn God's love, and He chooses to freely give it to us as sinners, we also can't do anything to lose God's love either. How cool is that? Romans 8:38-39 says, 'For I am persuaded that neither death nor life, nor angels nor principalities nor powers, nor things present nor things to come, nor height nor depth, nor any other created thing, shall be able to separate us from the love of God which is in Christ Jesus our Lord.' God's love is so strong for us that He wants to make sure that we don't lose it or forget it. The verse shows us that NOTHING can separate us from God's love.

When we have a full understanding of the Love of Father God, like we see in this week's verse, we will be filled with the fullness of God. That fullness keeps us planted and secure, as God's sons and daughters, so that the winds of life cannot blow us over."

Give students copy of lesson handout on pg. 23.

Say: "Every time you declare God's love or recite verses about God's love, you are growing your roots deeper and deeper. Remember, the deeper your roots are planted, the stronger you are, just like our flower was stronger when it was planted deeper."

Say Declaration and Prayer together.

Weekly Declaration: I plant myself in the amazing love of Father God. I don't have to do anything to earn His love. I just have to receive it.

Prayer: Father, Thank You for loving me SO much! I pray that I will continue to have a better understanding of how much You love me. Keep me rooted in Your great love so nothing in life can blow me over. In Jesus' name, amen!

*Extra Time: Have students color the Lesson 3 Coloring Sheet (pg. 24).

Lesson 3:
The Love of the Father

Verse
"That you, being rooted and grounded in love, may be able to comprehend [...] the width and length and depth and height- to know the love of Christ which passes knowledge; that you may be filled with all the fullness of God."
Ephesians 3:17-19

Declaration
I plant myself in the amazing love of Father God. I don't have to do anything to earn His love. I just have to receive it.

Prayer
Father, Thank You for loving me SO much! I pray that I will continue to have a better understanding of how much You love me. Keep me rooted in Your great love so nothing in life can blow me over. In Jesus' name, amen!

name

"That you, being rooted and grounded in love, may be able to comprehend … what is the width and length and depth and height- to know the love of Christ which passes knowledge; that you may be filled with all the fullness of God."

Ephesians 3:17-19

*Use to make copies for students

Scripture: John 8:31-32
Lesson Length: 45-50 minutes

THE TRUTH ABOUT GOD'S LOVE

Review
(3-5 mins)

Review last week's verse and declaration:
"That you, being rooted and grounded in love, may be able to comprehend ... what is the width and length and depth and height- to know the love of Christ which passes knowledge; that you may be filled with all the fullness of God."
Ephesians 3:17-19

- Show verse on the screen for those who weren't here last week.
- Ask students if they were able to memorize the verse. You can ask students to show a thumbs up or thumbs down to if they were able to memorize it and then ask students to recite it as a class, or recite it in groups of 2-3 if most already memorized it.
- Next, recite last week's Declaration together as a class:
  I plant myself in the amazing love of Father God. I don't have to do anything to earn His love. I just have to receive it.

"If you abide in My word, you are My disciples indeed. And you shall know the truth, and the truth shall make you free."

John 8:31-32

Introduce Today's Scripture: "If you abide in My word, you are My disciples indeed. And you shall know the truth, and the truth shall make you free." John 8:31-32

Ask: "What does it mean to be free?" *Give students 5-10 seconds to think of their answer and then have them share it with the person closest to them. Then, ask 1-2 students to share with the group.*

Say: "Being free means that nobody has control over you. Freedom is really important to God, and this verse tells us that if we 'abide,' or keep, God's word in our hearts, we will be made free.

We usually think of freedom as being free from another person's control or rules, but more importantly, God wants us to be free from the devil's lies. That is so important to God, because when we're not abiding, or keeping God's word in our hearts, we can easily start to believe lies that the devil tries to tell us.

The easiest lie that the devil always tries to tell us is that Father God does not love us. We must continue to read, speak, and keep God's word in our hearts so we won't believe any lies over the truth of God's word. God's word is our weapon against the enemy's lies."

Memory Verse
(8-10 mins)

"If you abide in My word, you are My disciples indeed. And you shall know the truth, and the truth shall make you free." John 8:31-32

- Use hand motions each time you memorize the words of the verse together. ***For younger students, you can memorize a smaller portion of the verse.**
- Optional Game: Write the verse on a chalkboard, dry erase board, or create slides with the verse. Say it together. Erase one word. Say it again. Erase another word and say it out loud together. Keep going until the whole verse is erased.
- Extension Games (optional): Split into 2 teams and race to see which team can have each member recite the verse the fastest or recite 'round robin' style with each student taking turns saying one word from the verse until they complete the entire verse together.

Craft: The Sword
(10-12 mins)

Directions: Have students create a sword to represent God's truths as the weapon to use against the enemy's lies.
- Younger students: Cut and Color the sword printout (pg. 33)
- Older students: Provide materials so they can create a sword out of paper, pipe cleaners, straws, pool noodles, etc.

Lesson + "I Believe" Activity
(10-15 mins)

Objective: Students will learn the importance of replacing lies with God's truths.

Directions: Have students use the swords from the craft so they can hold them up as they say the "I Believe" statements throughout the lesson.

Say: "God's truths are our weapon against the enemy's lies. John 8:44 tells us that the enemy, Satan, 'was a murderer from the beginning, and does not stand in the truth, because there is no truth in him. When he speaks a lie, he speaks from his own resources, for he is a liar and the father of it.' The easiest way for the enemy to attack us is with lies, because he is the father of lies. He tries to make us plant ourselves in lies instead of in God's love. But remember, we are rooted and grounded in God's love. In order to stay securely planted in God's love and freely receive the love of Father God, we need to know how to fight back when Satan tries to lie to us.

1 John 2:14 tells us, 'because you are strong, and the word of God abides in you, [...] you have overcome the wicked one.' It is showing us that abiding, or keeping God's word in our hearts, makes us strong to defeat the 'wicked one,' or enemy's, lies. There are several ways that the enemy tries to lie to us about God's love. He uses easy targets to make us think God loves us less than He really does. Remember, God is love, so love is the only feeling He has for us, and nothing can separate us from His love.

One area that keeps us from receiving the love of the Father is when we don't believe God's word about His love is true. This week's verse tells us, 'If you abide in My word, you are My disciples indeed. And you shall know the truth, and the truth shall make you free' John 8:31-32. We have to read and BELIEVE that God's word is TRUE about His love, so we can stay FREE from the devil's lies. Our weekly verses, declarations, and prayers help to fight off the enemy's lies. It is so important that we keep our roots planted in God's love.

If you ever feel like you don't know whether God loves you or not, or that you're not sure if God means what He says in the Bible, you can use the word of God to fight those doubts and confusion. For example, if I'm feeling doubts about something I read in the Bible, I'll realize that it is the enemy trying to lie to me to make me not trust God's word, so I loudly say, **'I believe**

that God's word is truth and His truth makes me free from the enemy's lies!' (John 8:32). When I declare God's word like this, it is my weapon attacking against the enemy's lie."

Exercise 1:
Say: "Let's practice together. Receiving the Father's love is so important so we can stay free from the enemy's lies. When you doubt that God really loves or cares about you, declare out loud: 'I believe that God created me in His own image, which is love!' (Genesis 1:26). This will fight off the attack of the enemy and remind you that God cares about you because He created you in His own image, which is love."

Have students stand up with their swords and recite together, "I believe that God created me in His own image, which is love!" multiple times. Remind them that this is what they can say when they feel like God doesn't love them.

Continue Lesson:
Say: "If Satan isn't able to make us believe that God doesn't love us, he tries to use another lie to convince us that God isn't the perfect Father to us. He easily does this by having us imagine that God is like our own fathers here on earth. Many of us have awesome dads that love us and care about us, but even the best dads on earth don't compare to how perfect our Father God is.

For example, maybe your dad works a lot and isn't home very often; you don't realize it, but you might start to think that Father God is too busy for you because He is helping others, like your earthly dad. Another example might be that we've seen our earthly dad get angry because of something we've done, so we start to believe that our Heavenly Father gets angry with us too.

The way we view our dads on earth can make us view Father God in the wrong way. We must know the truth so the enemy can't make us believe lies. The best way to know the truth about who God is, is to know who Jesus is. Colossians 1:15 says, Jesus 'is the image of the invisible God.' Jesus gave His life for us. Jesus gave us everything so we could live in freedom. That is a perfect love, just like the perfect love that Father God has for us."

Exercise 2:
Say: "When you start to think that God, your perfect Father who loves you deeply, is angry with you or is too busy for you, say: 'I believe God is my perfect father, who loves me so much, that He gave His son to die for me!' (John 3:16)."

Have students stand up with their swords and recite together multiple times. Remind them that this is what they can say when they feel like God is too busy for them or angry with them.

Continue Lesson:
Say: "Another lie that the enemy tells us is that we are not forgiven when we've done something wrong. Romans 3:23 says, 'for all have sinned and fall short of the glory of God.' We are all sinners, but Jesus came so we could be forgiven of ALL sins past, present, and future. We are not separated from God's love because of our sins. Jesus took our sins away at the cross."

Exercise 3:
Say: "When you think that your sin makes God love you less, say: 'I believe that death, nor life, nor anything can separate me from the love of God!' (Romans 8:38-39)."

Have students stand up with their swords and recite together multiple times. Remind them that this is what they can say when they feel like God loves them less because of their sins.

Continue Lesson:
Say: "Not only do we need to understand that we are forgiven, but it is important that we forgive ourselves and forgive others. When we have unforgiveness in our hearts, we are not free. Our anger or sadness with ourselves or other people gets in the way

30

of feeling the love of the Father. Whenever you feel angry or sad with yourself or somebody else, remember Romans 3:23 says, 'for all have sinned and fall short of the glory of God.' Nobody is perfect, so we must forgive ourselves and others because Christ already chose to forgive us all.

Now you have weapons to use against the enemy when he tries to lie to you about how much God loves you, tells you that God isn't the perfect Father, or tries to make you believe your sins are making God love you less. Always speak God's truths to fight back!"

**Weekly
Prayer and
Declaration**
(3-5 mins)

Give students copy of lesson handout on pg. 32.

Say: "Like we see in this week's verse, knowing the truth and being free is really important to God. The truth fights the enemy's lies so we can freely receive the love of the Father."

Say Declaration and Prayer together.

Weekly Declaration: I believe in the word of God and I am free from the lies of the enemy!

Prayer: Father, thank You that my freedom from lies is important to You. I pray that I continue to know how much You love me. Show me any ideas that I have about You that are incorrect, so I can see You as the perfect Father that You are. In Jesus' name, amen!

Lesson 4:
The Truth About God's Love

Verse
"If you abide in My word, you are My disciples indeed. And you shall know the truth, and the truth shall make you free." John 8:31-32

Declaration
I believe in the word of God and I am free from the lies of the enemy!

Prayer
Father, thank You that my freedom from lies is important to You. I pray that I continue to know how much You love me. Show me any ideas that I have about You that are incorrect, so I can see You as the perfect Father that You are. In Jesus' name, amen!

*Use to make copies for students

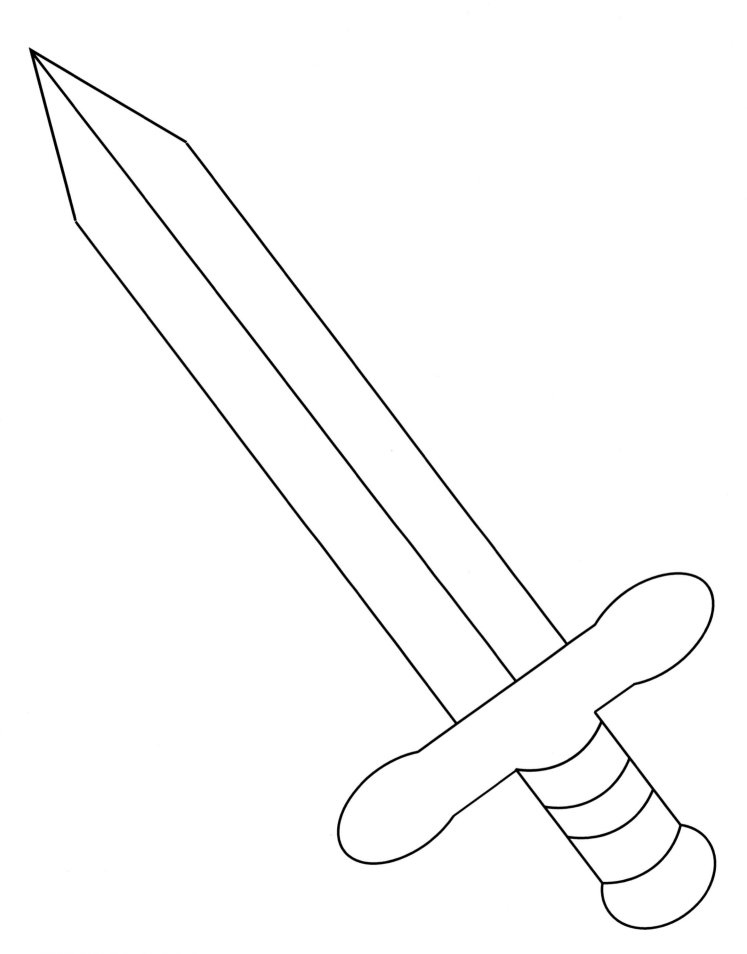

*Use to make copies for students

Scripture: 1 Corinthians 2:12
Lesson Length: 45-50 minutes

EMBRACING THE HOLY SPIRIT

Review
(3-5 mins)

Review last week's verse and declaration:
"If you abide in My word, you are My disciples indeed. And you shall know the truth, and the truth shall make you free." John 8:31-32

- Show verse on the screen for those who weren't here last week.
- Ask students if they were able to memorize the verse. You can ask students to show a thumbs up or thumbs down to if they were able to memorize it and then ask students to recite it as a class, or recite it in groups of 2-3 if most already memorized it.
- Next, recite last week's Declaration together as a class:
  I believe in the word of God and I am free from the lies of the enemy!

Intro
(4-6 mins)

Introduce Today's Scripture: "Now we have received, not the spirit of the world, but the Spirit who is from God, that we might know the things that have been freely given to us by God." 1 Corinthians 2:12

"Now we have received, not the spirit of the world, but the Spirit who is from God, that we might know the things that have been freely given to us by God."

1 Corinthians 2:12

Ask: "Does anybody know the name of the Spirit that comes from God that this verse is talking about?" *Let 1-2 students answer.*

Say: "The Spirit that comes from God is the Holy Spirit. The Holy Spirit is God. The Bible calls the Holy Spirit by several other names, because He does so much for us. For example, the Bible also calls Him the 'Holy Ghost, Spirit of Truth, Comforter, Helper, and Spirit of Adoption.'"

Ask: "What do you think are the things that are 'freely given to us by God' that this verse talks about?" *Give students 5-10 seconds to think of their answer and then have them share with the person closest to them. Then, ask 2-3 students to share their answers to the group.*

Say: "God freely gives us all things because He loves us so much. He freely gives us His love. He freely gave us His son at the cross. He freely gives us salvation. He freely gives us healing. He freely gives us help when we're in trouble, and so much more.

Romans 8:32 **says,** 'He who did not spare His own Son, but delivered Him up for us all, how shall He not with Him also freely give us all things?' This verse is asking if God gave us His most precious gift of all, His only son, Jesus, why would He choose to not freely give us all other things that are less valuable than Jesus' life? He wouldn't! God freely gives us everything we need because He loves us so much!"

Memory Verse

(8-10 mins)

"Now we have received, not the spirit of the world, but the Spirit who is from God, that we might know the things that have been freely given to us by God." 1 Corinthians 2:12

- Use hand motions each time you memorize the words of the verse together. ***For younger students, you can memorize a smaller portion of the verse.**
- Optional Game: Write the verse on a chalkboard, dry erase board, or create slides with the verse. Say it together. Erase one word. Say it again. Erase another word and say it out loud together. Keep going until the whole verse is erased.
- Extension Games (optional): Split into 2 teams and race to see which team can have each member recite the verse the fastest or recite 'round robin' style with each student taking turns saying one word from the verse until they complete the entire verse together.

Lesson

(8-10 mins)

Say: "We've been talking about our identity as sons and daughters in Christ, and the deep love of the Father these past few weeks. Knowing the Holy Spirit is the only way to have a close and intimate relationship with Father God as His sons and daughters. The Holy Spirit lives inside of us to help us hear God's voice clearly and understand all that He freely gives us.

Last week, we talked about how the enemy tries to make us believe lies. It is the Holy Spirit, that lives inside of us, who shows us God's truths to fight back against the enemy's lies. That is why one of the names for the Holy Spirit is 'Spirit of truth.' The Holy Spirit helps us understand God's word and truths, and shows us how to live out those truths in our lives so we can be free.

Jesus knew after He left earth to be with God that we would need help, so He prayed to the Father to give us the Holy Spirit. In John 14:16-17, Jesus says, 'And I will pray the Father, and He will give you another Helper, that He may abide with you forever-the Spirit of truth, whom the world cannot receive, because it neither sees Him nor knows Him; but you know Him, for He dwells with you and will be in you.' This verse tells us that the Holy Spirit is our Helper, and guides us to know the truth, because He is the Spirit of truth. It also says that the world cannot see Him, but that He dwells, or lives, inside us forever.

After we receive Jesus as our savior, the Holy Spirit comes to live in us to show us the love of the Father and help us understand what Jesus has freely given us. The Holy Spirit is also known as the Spirit of Adoption because He shows us that we are no longer orphans. We see in Romans 8:15: 'For you did not receive the spirit of bondage again to fear, but you received the Spirit of adoption by whom we cry out, "Abba, Father." It is the Holy Spirit who shows us that we are God's sons and daughters who can cry out to Him as our daddy God.

Remember, Jesus died on the cross for us so we would no longer be orphans, separated from Father God's love. The Holy Spirit came to live inside of us to continue showing us the love of the Father and strengthening our relationship with God by being our Spirit of truth and adoption. Sometimes we have trouble understanding what God is telling us through His word. That is when we need to ask the Holy Spirit to give us the power to fully understand God's word. He is always with us, so we can ask Him for help when we need it."

Activity:
"Crack
the Code"
Flashlight
(10-12 mins)

Objective: Demonstrate how the Holy Spirit guides us and helps us understand God's word.

Materials: Code Letters (pg. 45-49), tape, flashlights, Poster Board or Dry Erase Board to use for Secret Message Board

Directions: Students will use the help from their flashlights (Holy Spirit) to help them find the letters to crack the code (God's message to them).

SECRET MESSAGE: I can not earn the love of God, because He freely gives it to me.

To Prepare:
Copy and cut out the code letters (pg. 45-49) and tape them around the room. Create a "Secret Message Board" on a poster or dry erase board that you can organize the code letters on as the students find them. You can either tape the letters to it or write the letters on it as the students bring them up to you.
*See example layout of Secret Message Board on pg. 44

With the lights off, have students use flashlights to search around the room to find letters to spell out God's secret message to them. When a student finds a letter, they will bring it to the teacher to add to the Secret Message Board. The letters are ordered with a number in the top corner of the code letter.
• For a challenge, tape the letters in hidden spots, such as under tables, behind doors, etc.
• If you need to save time, fill in a few letters on the Secret Message Board before the game begins.

To Start:
Say: "Sometimes we feel like we can't hear God, or we are confused about what His word is saying to us. You can always ask the Holy Spirit to show you what God is saying, because He is the Spirit of Truth that lives inside of you. One of His important jobs is to guide us and show us the truth.

During this activity, we're going to demonstrate how the Holy Spirit shows us, or shines light, on God's word to us, by using flashlights to find God's special message to us. We have to find all of the letters and put them in order so we can crack the code.

When the game begins, you will use your flashlights to search around the room to find letters for the secret message from God. Each time you find a letter, run it up to the Secret Message Board so I can add it to the code. Make sure you bring one letter at a time before you start searching again."

Have students start in the center of the room with their flashlights. Turn off the lights and let students start searching for letters with their flashlights. They should find one letter at a time and run it up to the secret message board so the teacher can start organizing the letters based on the number in the top corner of the letter.

After all of the letters are found and they've cracked the code:
Say: "Just like the flashlights helped us find and hear God's message to us, the Holy Spirit does the same thing for us. He guides us and shows us the truths in God's word. The Holy Spirit lives inside of us to help guide us through life by revealing the Father's love to us, reminding us of our identity as sons and daughters, and giving us power to do the works that Jesus did.

Next week we'll talk more about the power that the Holy Spirit gives us so we can live like Jesus. Just remember, you can always ask the Holy Spirit for help when you need it, because He lives inside of you."

Clean up and start the next activity.

**Activity:
Holy Spirit
Message**
(5-7 mins)

Materials: Activity worksheet (pg. 43), writing materials

Say: "Because the Holy Spirit is the Spirit of Truth, and helps us hear God, we can ask the Holy Spirit to show us what God is saying to us by simply praying to Him at any time. The Holy Spirit is God living inside of us, so we talk to the Holy Spirit through prayer, just like we talk to God through prayer.

Let's ask the Holy Spirit to tell us what God wants us to know right now. We'll pray together and then I want you to write or draw anything that you think the Holy Spirit is saying or showing you. Repeat the prayer after me and then begin to write and draw on your worksheet."

Pray: Holy Spirit, I pray that you'll show me the truth that God wants me to know right now. Show me the message that God is saying to me today.

**Weekly
Prayer and
Declaration**
(3-5 mins)

Give students a copy of lesson handout on pg. 42.

Say: "Imagine that the Holy Spirit is a flashlight that lives inside of you that you can always turn on when you need help finding God's message to you."

Say Declaration and Prayer together.

Weekly Declaration: The Holy Spirit lives inside of me to show me the truth about Father God's love for me and my identity as His son/daughter.

Prayer: Father, thank You for giving me Your Holy Spirit to live inside of me. I receive the Holy Spirit now so I can continue to have a better understanding of Your love for me and my identity in You as Your son/daughter. In Jesus' name, amen!

Lesson 5:
Embracing the Holy Spirit

Verse
"Now we have received, not the spirit of the world, but the Spirit who is from God, that we might know the things that have been freely given to us by God."
1 Corinthians 2:12

Declaration
The Holy Spirit lives inside of me to show me the truth about Father God's love for me and my identity as His Son/Daughter.

Prayer
Father, thank You for giving me Your Holy Spirit to live inside of me. I receive the Holy Spirit now so I can continue to have a better understanding of Your love for me and my identity in You as Your son/daughter. In Jesus' name, amen!

*Use to make copies for students

Ask the Holy Spirit to show you what God is saying to you right now. Write it or draw it below.

Name: _____

Secret Message Board Layout

| 1 | | 2 3 | | 4 | | 5 | | 6 7 | | 8 | | 9 | | 10 11 | | 12 | | 13 14 | | 15 | | 16 17 | | 18 | | 19 20 |

, 21 22 23 | | 24 25 26 | | 27 28 | | 29 30 | | 31 32 | | 33 | | 34 35 | | 36 | | 37 38 | | 39 40 | | 41 42 | | 43

44 45 | | 46 47 | | 48 49 | .

1 i	2 c
3 a	4 n
5 n	6 o
7 t	8 e
9 a	10 r

*Copy & cut-out letters for activity

11 n	12 t
13 h	14 e
15 l	16 o
17 v	18 e
19 o	20 f

*Copy & cut-out letters for activity

21 G	22 o
23 d	24 b
25 e	26 c
27 a	28 u
29 s	30 e

*Copy & cut-out letters for activity

31 H	32 e
33 f	34 r
35 e	36 e
37 l	38 y
39 g	40 i

*Copy & cut-out letters for activity

41 v	42 e
43 s	44 i
45 t	46 t
47 o	48 m
49 e	

Scripture: Acts 1:8
Lesson Length: 45-50 minutes

BAPTIZED IN THE HOLY SPIRIT

Review last week's verse and declaration:
"Now we have received, not the spirit of the world, but the Spirit who is from God, that we might know the things that have been freely given to us by God." 1 Corinthians 2:12

- Show verse on the screen for those who weren't here last week.
- Ask students if they were able to memorize the verse. You can ask students to show a thumbs up or thumbs down to if they were able to memorize it and then ask students to recite it as a class, or recite it in groups of 2-3 if most already memorized it.
- Next, recite last week's Declaration together as a class:
  The Holy Spirit lives inside of me to show me the truth about Father God's love for me and my identity as His son/daughter.

Introduce Today's Scripture: "But you shall receive power when the Holy Spirit has come upon you; and you shall be witnesses to Me [...] to the end of the earth."
Acts 1:8

"But you shall receive power when the Holy Spirit has come upon you; and you shall be witnesses to Me [...] to the end of the earth."

Acts 1:8

Ask: "Think about what we learned last week. How does the Holy Spirit help us?" *Give students 5-10 seconds to think of their answer. Have them share with the person closest to them. Then, ask 1-3 students to share with the group.*

Say: "The Holy Spirit is the Spirit of Truth and the Spirit of Adoption. He shines light on God's word for us and reminds us that we are sons and daughters of Father God."

Ask: "Today's verse says we will receive power when the Holy Spirit has come upon us. What do we think that means?" *Let 1-2 students answer.*

Say: "In this verse, Jesus is speaking to His disciples. He's telling them that they will have power to be His witnesses everywhere they go on Earth when the Holy Spirit is upon them. Since we also have the Holy Spirit in us, we are witnesses of Jesus too. Being a witness of Jesus means that we go around and do the works that Jesus did while He was on earth such as sharing the love of the Father, healing the sick, and setting captives free from the enemy's lies."

Memory Verse

(8-10 mins)

"But you shall receive power when the Holy Spirit has come upon you; and you shall be witnesses to Me [...] to the end of the earth." Acts 1:8

- Use hand motions each time you memorize the words of the verse together. ***For younger students, you can memorize a smaller portion of the verse.**
- Optional Game: Write the verse on a chalkboard, dry erase board, or create slides with the verse. Say it together. Erase one word. Say it again. Erase another word and say it out loud together. Keep going until the whole verse is erased.
- Extension Games (optional): Split into 2 teams and race to see which team can have each member recite the verse the fastest or recite 'round robin' style with each student taking turns saying one word from the verse until they complete the entire verse together.

Lesson

(8-10 mins)

Say: "The Holy Spirit helps us in many ways. The Holy Spirit shines light on God's word for us because He is the Spirit of truth. He also gives us the Spirit of adoption, which makes us sons and daughters of Father God. Another way the Holy Spirit helps us is by giving us power to do the works of Jesus.

Acts 10:38 says, 'God anointed Jesus of Nazareth with the Holy Spirit and with power, who went about doing good and healing all who were oppressed by the devil, for God was with Him.' This verse shows us the Holy Spirit gave power to Jesus to do good, heal the sick, and set captives free from the devil's lies. Since the Holy Spirit gives us power to be witnesses of Jesus, we can go and do exactly what He did on earth.

Another verse that tells us what Jesus did on earth is Luke 4:18-19. In this verse, Jesus tells us, 'He has sent Me to heal the brokenhearted, to proclaim liberty to the captives and recovery of sight to the blind, to set at liberty those who are oppressed; to proclaim the acceptable year of the Lord.' This shows us again what we need to do as we live on earth as witnesses of Jesus:

do good, heal the sick, and free the captives [or prisoners] from the enemy's lies.   The only way we can do the same works of Jesus is by being baptized in the Holy Spirit so we have heavenly power.

Our verse today says we will receive power when the Holy Spirit has come upon us. Another way to say this is that we will receive power when we are baptized in the Holy Spirit. When we think about baptism, we think about being dunked in water. When we're baptized in the Holy Spirit, it's like we are dunked in the Holy Spirit and filled with heavenly power. In Luke 3:16, John the Baptist said that we would be baptized with the Holy Spirit and fire. Doesn't that sound powerful? When somebody has fire in them, it means they are passionate and powerful! We can have the fire of God inside of us to do the same works and miracles that Jesus did on earth, just by asking Father God to be baptized in the Holy Spirit.

God tells us that He freely gives us the baptism of the Holy Spirit when we ask. In Luke 11:9-13, He makes it a point to show us how much He wants to give us the Holy Spirit. It says, 'So I say to you, ask, and it will be given to you; seek, and you will find; knock, and it will be opened to you. For everyone who asks receives, and he who seeks finds, and to him who knocks, it will be opened. If a son asks for bread from any father among you, will he give him a stone? Or if he asks for a fish, will he give him a serpent instead of a fish? Or if he asks for an egg, will he offer him a scorpion? If you then, being evil, know how to give good gifts to your children, how much more will your heavenly Father give the Holy Spirit to those who ask Him!'

These verses show us that we just need to ask God, and He will give us the baptism of the Holy Spirit! God made it a point to show us that the Holy Spirit is a gift, and it is a gift that God WANTS to give us. We just need to ask him.

We see in another verse in Acts 19:5-6 that Paul prayed and laid hands on a group of people, and they were baptized in the Holy Spirit. It says, 'When they heard this, they were baptized in the name of the Lord Jesus. And when Paul had laid hands on them, the Holy Spirit came upon them, and they spoke with tongues and prophesied.' So not only can we pray for ourselves to be baptized in the Holy Spirit, but after we have the power of the Holy Spirit, we can also lay hands and pray for others to be baptized in the Holy Spirit."

Activity: Plugged into the Spirit

(4-6 mins)

Objective: Demonstrate how the power of the Holy Spirit gives us the power to do the works of Jesus.

Materials: fan with a power cord

Start with the fan unplugged, but don't let the students know that it is unplugged.

Say: "Imagine that we are fans. When we are around others, we are able to help them stay cool. Watch as I turn the switch on. You will be able to feel the fan."
Turn the fan switch on. Ask students why they think it isn't working. After they tell you it isn't plugged in, plug in the fan.

Say: "Now the fan is plugged in to the power. When we're baptized in the Holy Spirit, it is like we're plugged in to His power. Watch as I turn the fan on now."
Turn on the fan.

Ask: "Can you feel the fan now?"

Say: "Just like the fan doesn't have power to cool us off unless it is plugged into a power source, we don't have power to do the works of Jesus unless we are plugged in to the Holy Spirit's power. He is always with us, so we can plug into His power anytime we ask. When we have His power, we can help others by doing good, sharing the Father's love, healing the sick, and freeing the captives from the enemy's lies. We can use the Spirit of truth to help others become free, just like we use His truths to keep ourselves free from the enemy's lies. We can lay hands and pray for others when we're filled with the Holy Spirit's power."

Have students partner up, so they can pray for each other.

Say: "First, we're going to ask the Father for the baptism of the Holy Spirit, because remember, He tells us, 'how much more will your heavenly Father give the Holy Spirit to those who ask Him!' So pray the same words after me."

Have students put their hands on their hearts or bellies and repeat after you:

Pray: Father, Baptize me now with the Holy Spirit and with fire, so that Your power can flow through me and I can do Your works and miracles like Jesus. In Jesus' name, amen!

Say: "Next we're going to lay hands on your partner and pray for them, just like Paul laid hands to pray for people to receive the baptism of the Holy Spirit. One person will start. Then, we'll switch and pray again so the other person can pray."

Pray: Father, Baptize [name] now with the Holy Spirit and with fire, so that Your power can flow through them to do Your works and miracles like Jesus. In Jesus' name, amen!

Repeat for second partner.

Weekly Prayer and Declaration
(3-5 mins)

Give students a copy of lesson handout on pg. 58.

Say: "Remember, you can always ask the Holy Spirit for His power to do good by sharing the love of the Father, healing the sick, and setting the captives free, just like Jesus did."

Say Declaration and Prayer together.

Weekly Declaration: The Holy Spirit gives me power to do good works by sharing the Father's love, healing the sick, and setting the captives free like Jesus.

Prayer: Father, Baptize me now with the Holy Spirit and with fire, so that Your power can flow through me, and I can do Your works and miracles like Jesus. In Jesus' name, amen!

Lesson 6:
Baptized in the Holy Spirit

Verse
"But you shall receive power when the Holy Spirit has come upon you; and you shall be witnesses to Me [...] to the end of the earth." Acts 1:8

Declaration
The Holy Spirit gives me power to do good by sharing the Father's love, healing the sick, and setting the captives free like Jesus.

Prayer
Father, Baptize me now with the Holy Spirit and with fire, so that Your power can flow through me, and I can do Your works and miracles like Jesus. In Jesus' name, amen!

Scripture: 2 Corinthians 5:17
Lesson Length: 45-50 minutes

OUR NEW IDENTITY IN CHRIST

Review last week's verse and declaration:
"But you shall receive power when the Holy Spirit has come upon you; and you shall be witnesses to Me [...] to the end of the earth." Acts 1:8

- Show verse on the screen for those who weren't here last week.
- Ask students if they were able to memorize the verse. You can ask students to show a thumbs up or thumbs down to if they were able to memorize it and then ask students to recite it as a class, or recite it in groups of 2-3 if most already memorized it.
- Next, recite last week's Declaration together as a class:
  The Holy Spirit gives me power to do good by sharing the Father's love, healing the sick, and setting the captives free like Jesus.

Introduce Today's Scripture: "Therefore, if anyone is in Christ, he is a new creation; old things have passed away; behold, all things have become new." 2 Corinthians 5:17

"Therefore, if anyone is in Christ, he is a new creation; old things have passed away; behold, all things have become new."

2 Corinthians 5:17

Say: "When we are born again, and the Holy Spirit comes to live inside of us, we are new creations in Christ. We are a new version of ourselves, and we are no longer the old version of ourselves. Think about some products that you use today. Let's look at how they compare to the old versions."

Choose a few items to show as an example of old vs. new. You can print out pictures, show videos, or bring the actual items to show. Examples: Atari vs. Xbox, Walkman headphones vs. airpods, landline vs. cell phones, audio difference between record players and streamed music, old television vs. new television, fashion trends, etc.

Discuss together why the new items are better. Mention that they look better, function better, are more popular, etc.

Say: "Just like we see with these items, we are the newer and better item when we are in Christ. Like today's verse says, our old self passes away and we become new."

Memory Verse
(8-10 mins)

"Therefore, if anyone is in Christ, he is a new creation; old things have passed away; behold, all things have become new." 2 Corinthians 5:17

- Use hand motions each time you memorize the words of the verse together. ***For younger students, you can memorize a smaller portion of the verse.**
- Optional Game: Write the verse on a chalkboard, dry erase board, or create slides with the verse. Say it together. Erase one word. Say it again. Erase another word and say it out loud together. Keep going until the whole verse is erased.
- Extension Games (optional): Split into 2 teams and race to see which team can have each member recite the verse the fastest or recite 'round robin' style with each student taking turns saying one word from the verse until they complete the entire verse together.

Lesson
(8-10 mins)

Say: "How do you see yourself? Is it the same way God sees you? It is so important that we see ourselves the way God sees us. Like today's verse says, God sees us as a new creation. He sees us as righteous sons and daughters, because He no longer views our past, present, or future sins. We are a new creation in Him. Hebrews 10:17 says, 'Their sins and lawless deeds I will remember no more.' This verse reminds us that God chooses not to see our sins, but instead sees us as new creations in Christ.

In Ephesians 1:6, it says, 'He made us accepted in the Beloved.' Because of God's beloved Son, Jesus, we are accepted. Just think about what it means to be accepted. When you're accepted with your friends and family, you are loved and appreciated for who you are. You don't have to pretend to be something else. We are new creations in Christ, and we don't have to pretend to be anything else, because God sees us as He sees Christ. His beloved sons and daughters. Do you see yourself as God's beloved child?

Remember, the enemy is the father of lies, and tries to make us believe lies about ourselves and about God. Sometimes we listen to what another person says about us, like a teacher or a friend, instead of what God says. Maybe they make you feel like you're not good enough or you're not accepted for who you are. That is the enemy lying to you. You are a new creation in Christ and accepted in the beloved. Just like the newest Xbox or new cell phone, you're like the brand new product of God that is way better than the old product.

Ephesians 2:10 says, 'For we are His workmanship, created in Christ Jesus for good works, which God prepared beforehand that we should walk in them.' To be God's 'workmanship' means we are his works of art that He put all of His love into. He created us for good works and sees us as His workmanship, or masterpieces. We know that God sees us this way because in 2 Corinthians 5:21, it says, 'For He made [Jesus] who knew no sin, to be sin for us, that we might become the righteousness of God in Him.' Because of what Jesus did at the cross, God now calls us righteous! To be righteous, means to be excellent and like royalty. God sees us this way because he chooses not to see our sins, but instead sees us like He sees Jesus.

Again, how do you see yourself? Do you believe that you are righteous? If you don't see yourself as God sees you, as righteous and a beautiful new creation, then ask yourself why. Where is the enemy lying to you? Remember, the Holy Spirit helps us to hear God and to show us our identity as sons and daughters, because He is the Spirit of Truth and Adoption. So, instead of believing the lie, stand up and say, 'I'm a new creation and accepted in the beloved! God chooses not to see my sins and calls me righteous!'

Picture yourself as a caterpillar, who goes into a cocoon and comes out as a new, beautiful butterfly. That is exactly how God sees you. You are a new, beautiful butterfly, because of what Jesus did at the cross. Don't forget, it brings God so much joy to be your Heavenly Father, because you are His righteous child!"

Optional: Show a video clip of a butterfly hatching from a cocoon.

Craft: Newest Creation
(10-12 mins)

Objective: Students will decorate shoes or a butterfly to symbolize a "new creation" or "workmanship," just like God sees them.

Materials: Shoe and Butterfly printouts (pg. 65-66), materials to decorate with: glue, glitter, pompoms, colored pencils, yarn, pipe cleaners, etc.

Say: "We are God's new creations. You're the workmanship, or piece of art, that God created. You can choose to create an example of a new creation by decorating a butterfly or the newest pair of shoes. Remember to make it look like a brand new masterpiece, because that is what You are to God!"

Weekly Prayer and Declaration
(3-5 mins)

Give students a copy of lesson handout on pg. 64.

Say: "We are new creations in Christ. Sometimes we forget how God really sees us. This week, we're going to declare our new identity in Christ."

Say Declaration and Prayer together.

Weekly Declaration: I am accepted in the Beloved. God sees me as righteous and a new creation.

Prayer: Father, continue to show me who I am in You. Thank You for choosing not to see my sin, but to see me as a righteous new creation. Help me to see myself as You see me. In Jesus' name, amen!

Lesson 7:
Our New Identity In Christ

Verse
"Therefore, if anyone is in Christ, he is a new creation; old things have passed away; behold, all things have become new."
2 Corinthians 5:17

Declaration
I am accepted in the Beloved. God sees me as righteous and a new creation.

Prayer
Father, continue to show me who I am in You. Thank You for choosing not to see my sin, but to see me as a righteous new creation. Help me to see myself as You see me. In Jesus' name, amen!

*Use to make copies for students

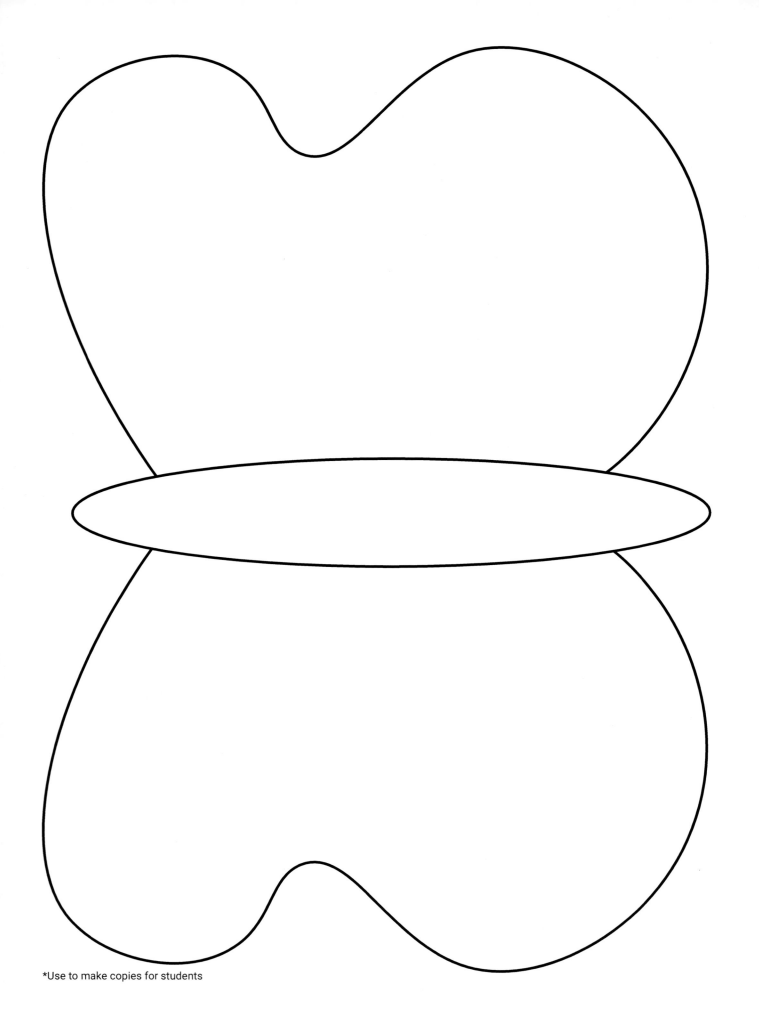

*Use to make copies for students

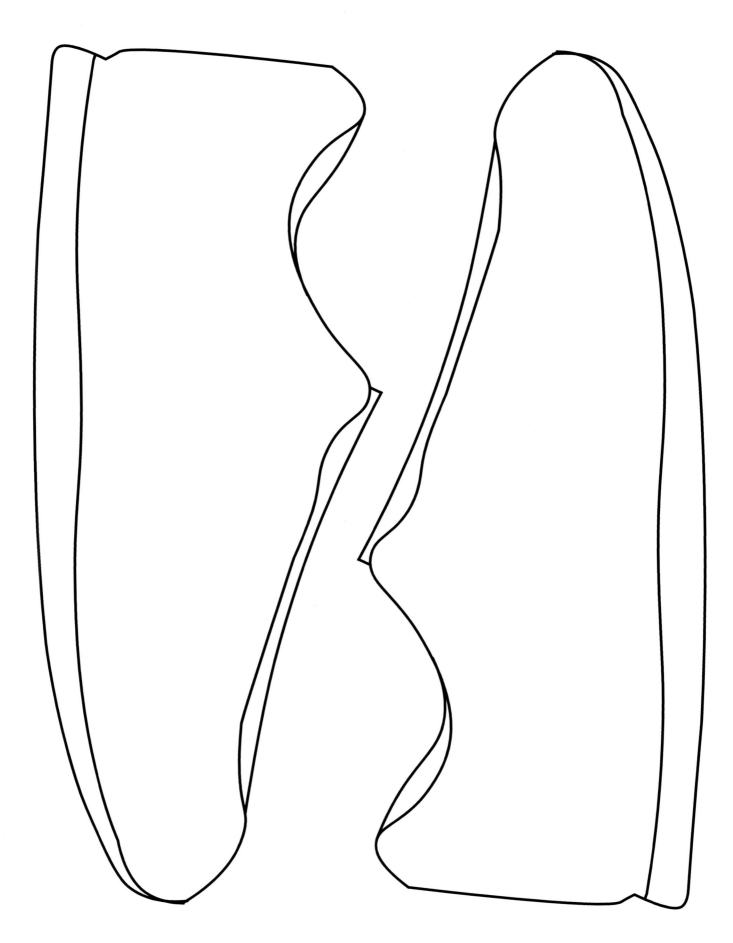

*Use to make copies for students

Scripture: Genesis 1:28
Lesson Length: 45-50 minutes

Advancing the Kingdom

Review
(3-5 mins)

Review last week's verse and declaration:
"Therefore, if anyone is in Christ, he is a new creation; old things have passed away; behold, all things have become new."
2 Corinthians 5:17

- Show verse on the screen for those who weren't here last week.
- Ask students if they were able to memorize the verse. You can ask students to show a thumbs up or thumbs down to if they were able to memorize it and then ask students to recite it as a class, or recite it in groups of 2-3 if most already memorized it.
- Next, recite last week's Declaration together as a class:
  I am accepted in the Beloved. God sees me as righteous and a new creation.

"Then God blessed them, and God said to them, "Be fruitful and multiply; fill the earth and subdue it."

Genesis 1:28

Intro
(2-4 mins)

Introduce Today's Scripture: "Then God blessed them, and God said to them, "Be fruitful and multiply; fill the earth and subdue it." Genesis 1:28

Say: "Several weeks ago, we studied Genesis 1:27 which said, 'So God created man in His own image; in the image of God He created him.' Right after God created man to be like Him, God told man why he was created. This is also called purpose.

In today's verse, we see God explain man's purpose by saying, 'Be fruitful and multiply; fill the earth and subdue it.' Genesis 1:28. This is God telling man what his purpose is on earth, and we still have the same purpose today. This shows us exactly what God planned for us to do at the beginning of the world."

Memory Verse
(4-6 mins)

"Then God blessed them, and God said to them, "Be fruitful and multiply; fill the earth and subdue it." Genesis 1:28

Save time for Stations Activity
• Use hand motions each time you memorize the words of the verse together.

68

Say: "God sees us as new creations, created in His own image. He created us to be fruitful, multiply, and fill the earth. To be fruitful, means others can see your "fruit," or your blessings, that God gives you as His new creation. The Holy Spirit living inside of us is what gives us our fruits, or blessings, for others to see. The fruits that this verse talks about, are the same fruits that Jesus showed us when He was here on earth: knowing the love of the Father, being healed, and being free from the enemy's lies.

The verse also tells us to multiply and fill the earth. This means God wants us to grow, or advance, His heavenly kingdom here on earth until it is filled with it. Think of it like this, say I LOVE the beach so much, that I want to bring it here to the church. I could plant palm trees everywhere, and maybe even buy tons of sand to lay around the building so it feels like a beach when I walk outside. I could give everybody tropical shirts, and pass out coconuts and sunscreen. Maybe I would even add a pool and play ocean noises on a speaker. This would be an example of advancing, or growing, a beach atmosphere around me."

Ask: "So, what do you think we can do to advance, or grow, God's heavenly kingdom here around us?" *Give students 5-10 seconds to think of their answer. Have them share with the person closest to them. Then, have 1-3 students share with the group.*

Say: "Jesus showed us what it looked like to advance, or grow, the kingdom here on earth. He did good works by spreading the message about the Father's love, healing the sick, and setting the captives free with God's truths. Jesus tells us this in Luke 4:18. He says, 'The Spirit of the Lord is upon Me, because He has anointed Me to preach the gospel to the poor; he has sent Me to heal the brokenhearted, to proclaim liberty to the captives and recovery of sight to the blind, and to set at liberty those who are oppressed [believing lies].'

Jesus knew exactly what needed to be done to advance the kingdom while He was here, and He demonstrated it for us, so we could continue to advance the kingdom after He left earth.

Remember, He gave us the Holy

Spirit when He left so we could use His power to continue doing His works.

In Matthew 10:7-8, Jesus tells us this: 'And as you go, preach, saying, 'The kingdom of heaven is at hand.' Heal the sick, cleanse the lepers, raise the dead, cast out demons. Freely you have received, freely give.' He wants us to be baptized in the Holy Spirit and fire, so we can perform and do the same works that He did on earth: to share the love of the father, heal the sick, and set captives free from the enemy's lies. He tells us that we've freely received these things, so we should freely give them to others.

This will grow God's kingdom, because others will start to be fruitful when we use our fruits to help them in these ways. When those people become fruitful, because they start to know the deep love of the Father, are healed, and free from the enemy's lies, they will then help others be fruitful. It is like a cycle, because the more people we share our fruits with, they will then start to share their fruits with even more people. This is how we can be fruitful, multiply, and fill the earth to grow God's kingdom here on earth. It is our job and our purpose to show our fruitfulness as new creations of God, and to help others be fruitful.

Knowing the love of the father, so we can see ourselves as His new creations, helps us to share His love with others. It also helps us to bear fruits, by receiving our blessings from the Holy Spirit. Remember, the Holy Spirit is our spirit of truth and adoption, so we must always listen to Him so we can continue to understand God's deep love for us. Don't forget, John 3:16 tells us, 'For God so loved the world that He gave His only begotten son,' Jesus, to die on the cross for us. He did this so we could go back to His original plan from the beginning, by making us new creations in Christ that can advance His kingdom here on earth with the power of the Holy Spirit."

Activity: "Advancing the Kingdom" Stations

(15-18 mins)

Objective: Students will demonstrate what it looks like to advance the kingdom in different station activities.

Materials: Package of heart stickers, Heal the Sick handout (pg. 74), Keychain handout (pg. 75), decorating materials: colors, glue, glitter, pompoms, etc.

Say: "Remember, the reason we were created is to advance God's kingdom by being fruitful, multiplying, and filling the earth. Jesus said we were freely given the love of the Father, healing, and freedom from the enemy's lies, so we must also freely give those things to others. Our purpose is to share the love of the father, heal the sick, and set the captives free from the enemy's lies. This is how we can advance God's kingdom here on earth.

First, let's pray for power from the Holy Spirit, because He gives us the power to do the works of Jesus. Pray after me:

Father, give me the Holy Spirit and fire to do the same works as Jesus. In Jesus' name, amen!"

Next, explain the three different stations, and have students split up evenly to start at different station. They should take their workbooks with them and spend 3-5 minutes at each station. Make sure to track time and have them switch stations every 3-5 minutes.

Station 1: Sharing the Father's Love
Objective: Students will demonstrate what it looks like to advance the kingdom by sharing the love of the Father with those around them.
Materials: Heart Stickers

Give each student 2-4 stickers so they can go around the room, or into the hallway, to share the love of the Father with others by giving them a heart sticker. Have them practice saying, "God loves you so much" or "God so loves you, that He gave His only son to die for you." They will use a few minutes to go around to 2-4 people to share God's love by giving them a heart sticker and telling them that God loves them.

Station 2: Healing the Sick
Objective: Students will decorate the prayer for healing that they can give to somebody in need this week.
Materials: Healing Handout (pg. 74), decorating materials: colors, yarn, scissors, glue, glitter, pompoms, etc.

Station 3: The Key to Setting the Captives Free
Objective: Students will remind themselves that the key to freedom is knowing God's truths by decorating a keychain about God's truths.
Materials: Keychain handout (pg. 75), coloring materials

Students can write a Bible verse, draw a picture, or anything else they want to represent the key to freedom, which is God's word.

Give students a copy of lesson handout on pg. 73.

Say: "Our job, or purpose, is to share the love of the Father, heal the sick, and set the captives free from the enemy's lies. Remember, God gave us the Holy Spirit to help us do this job. This week, we're going to pray that God continues to show us the power we have access to through the Holy Spirit, so we can advance His kingdom."

Say Declaration and Prayer together.

Weekly Declaration: God gave me the Holy Spirit and fire so I can advance His kingdom by sharing His love, healing the sick, and setting the captives free from the enemy's lies.

Prayer: Father, Thank You for choosing me from the beginning to advance Your kingdom. Let Your love shine through me so others can see it. Fill me with the Holy Spirit and fire so I can do the same works that Jesus did here on earth. In Jesus' name, amen!

Weekly Prayer and Declaration
(3-5 mins)

Lesson 8:
Advancing the Kingdom

Verse
"Then God blessed them, and God said to them, "Be fruitful and multiply; fill the earth and subdue it."
Genesis 1:28

Declaration
God gave me the Holy Spirit and fire so I can advance His kingdom by sharing His love, healing the sick, and setting the captives free from the enemy's lies.

Prayer
Father, Thank You for choosing me from the beginning to advance Your kingdom. Let Your love shine through me so others can see it. Fill me with the Holy Spirit and fire so I can do the same works that Jesus did here on earth. In Jesus' name, amen!

*Use to make copies for students

GOD WANTS YOU IN PERFECT HEALTH

Father, You love us so much that You sent Jesus to die for us, so we can be in perfect health. Thank You for releasing Your HEALING right now, in Jesus name! Amen!

GOD WANTS YOU IN PERFECT HEALTH

Father, You love us so much that You sent Jesus to die for us, so we can be in perfect health. Thank You for releasing Your HEALING right now, in Jesus name! Amen!

*Use to make copies for students

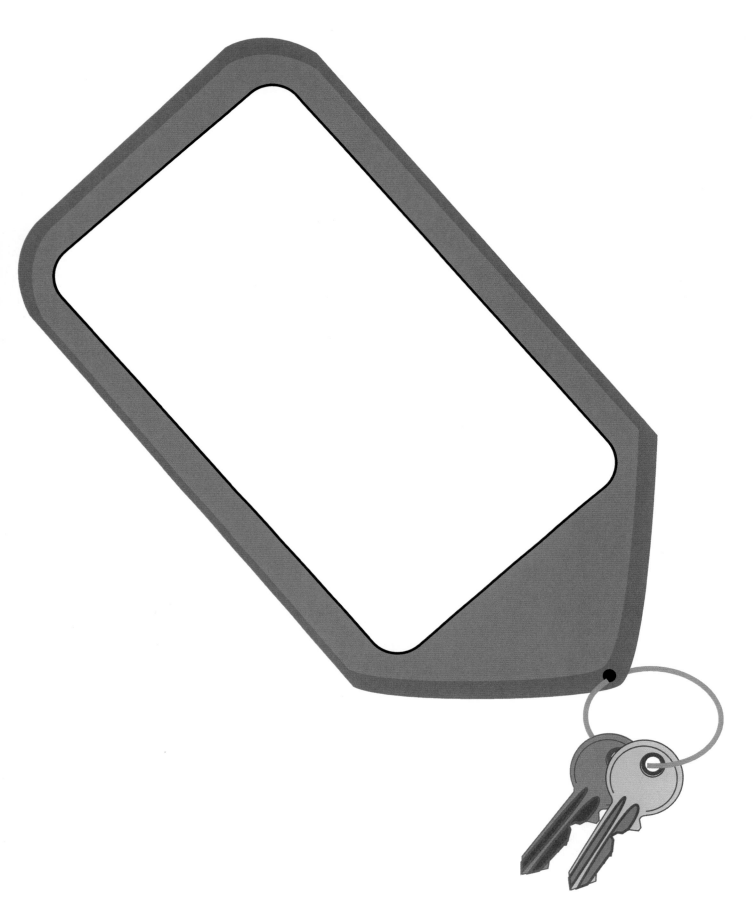

*Use to make copies for students

Made in the USA
Coppell, TX
08 February 2023

12439575R00050